County
DURHAM
A Rare Insight

First Edition 2020

ISBN 978 1 8380086 0 4

The information in this book is true and complete to the best of our knowledge. All recommendations are made without any guarantee on the part of the Publisher, who also disclaims any liability incurred in connection with the use of specific details or content within this book.

All rights reserved. No part of this book may be reproduced or transmitted in any form or by any means, electronic or mechanical, including photo-copying, scanning, recording or by any information storage and retrieval system, without permission from the Publisher in writing.

© 2020 Araf Chohan

British Library Cataloguing-in-Publication Data

A catalogue record for this book is available from the British Library.

Published by Destinworld Publishing Ltd.

www.destinworld.com

Cover design by Ken Leeder

CONTENTS

Introduction 5

Dedication 7

Central Durham 11

North Durham 26

East Durham & The Coast 47

South Durham 57

West Durham & Teesdale 86

Durham City 99

Acknowledgements 126

DURHAM - A RARE INSIGHT

INTRODUCTION

County Durham contains a wondrous array of villages, small country towns and different landscapes. From the coast in the east to the Durham Dales in the west, the glory of Durham City and the many villages and towns which exist because of the industries which once defined the county.

Durham's rich history is second to none, from Roman times to being at the forefront of the rise of Industrial Britain.

The towns and villages range from pretty country market towns to ex pit villages which have gone through so many post-industrial changes, giving County Durham a very diverse environment. It is a county full of surprises and architectural delights and at its heart is the capital of Durham, an ancient and beautiful cathedral city.

The city of Durham is not just the county seat but is a historic market town on a beautiful setting on a loop of the River Wear. It is a World Heritage Site which was inscribed on the list by UNESCO in 1986. Durham Cathedral is one of Europe's greatest medieval buildings, and contains the shrine of St Cuthbert, one of England's most revered saints. It also contains one of the finest Norman castles in Britain at the centre of this lovely small city.

Durham University is a world-class institution with 12,000 students, making today's population a vibrant mix of worldwide nationalities, adding to the feeling of this being a thriving and young city despite its obvious age.

The smaller towns of the county are a collection of small but distinctive urban areas, with ancient markets and post-industrial pit villages. County Durham is unique in Britain for it's rural as well as it's urban diversity.

Turning to this book, towns such as Consett, Chester Le Street, Bishop Auckland or Spennymoor and scores of pretty villages too numerous to name are seen here in their Edwardian heyday. Dominated by horse drawn vehicles and in some towns by electric trams and early motor vehicles, these images show a world long gone, a quaint world that is now consigned to history.

This was a time that was not that far away, as it was the world of our grandparents and great grandparents but still seems so distant to us in the 21st Century.

INTRODUCTION

As you will see, town centres were once thriving places of business, and the edges of the towns were bustling industrial centres usually focussed around a coal mine and its railway infrastructure. It is a stark contrast to today, however the many rural scenes also shown in the book have not changed much at all and show off the beauty of Durham.

The wonderful images in this book come from my own personal postcard collection, which I stared when only 14 way back in 1968.

Deltiology, or picture postcard collecting, has been a passion of mine which has resulted in various books on my home town of Middlesbrough, as well as others on Darlington, the North York Moors and London. This book has been a great pleasure for me to have been involved in as County Durham holds a warm place in my heart.

The boundary between County Durham and Yorkshire is the River Tees which I can see from my window, and can cross via the Transporter bridge. Durham is well known to me and it's towns and villages seen here via my old postcards bring to life a more sedate and elegant bygone age that I hope will bring pleasure to all who open these pages.

Araf Chohan, October 2020

DEDICATION

For Bari Tariq Khan Chohan my beloved Big Brother

Dedications by their very name imply remembrance and quite often sadness at the loss of a family member or a close friend, as is the case here in this book.

This book on County Durham is especially poignant and very close to my heart, as my very first Edwardian postcards were given to me by Bari in 1966 and were of Durham City and Jesmond Dene. These three cards were the start of my lifelong love of Edwardian postcard collecting and were the beginnings of what was to become a vast collection; they are the most treasured in my collection being the first and because they were given to me by my brother all those years ago.

Although he was Born in Nottingham on September 30th 1950, he was brought back to our family home in Grange Road, Middlesbrough as a baby in 1951, and sadly he was also brought back to Middlesbrough in January 2020 upon his demise as he had passed away in Dubai on 28th of December 2019 aged 69. He was a BORO BOY all his life and was laid to rest close to other family members here in his beloved hometown of Middlesbrough.

Thank you BARI, my caring and loving big brother, for those very first cards and you will always, always be in my heart, remembered and loved forever.

A sad and grieving brother,

Araf Khan Chohan

DURHAM - A RARE INSIGHT

DURHAM - A RARE INSIGHT

DURHAM - A RARE INSIGHT

CENTRAL DURHAM

The heart of Brancepeth village looking towards the entrance to Brancepeth Castle which dates to the Norman period. Much of it was rebuilt in the 14th century, and then in the 19th century when it became the home of Viscount Boyne.

The road crossing the scene is today the A690 which links Durham to Crook. The row of cottages still stands.

Brancepeth Castle from the Park

Brancepeth Castle is one of County Durham's most impressive buildings. The first castle was built after the Norman Conquest, with much of the present building dating to the 19th century when Viscount Boyne, who later became Baron Brancepeth, had it rebuilt.

The deer park surrounding the castle, seen here with stags looking towards the camera, was turned into the well-regarded Brancepeth Golf Course in 1924.

Brancepeth Colliery

Brancepeth Colliery was actually located near to Willington. It was opened in 1840 and survived until 1967 when the buildings and workers were made redundant. In April 1896 an explosion in "A" pit here caused the death of 20 men and boys working on the seam.

Darlington Road. Chilton. 3769

Despite its origins in the 1090s, Chilton as we know it today emerged as a mining town. By the time of this picture in the early 1900s, it had grown a sizeable population which was largely employed by the mine, and its situation on the main road between Darlington and Durham gave these shops plenty of passing trade.

Since 2005 the A167 bypasses the town, and the road in this picture is known as Durham Road. All of the buildings in view, including the distant Windlestone Methodist Church, are still standing. However, the Victorian shop fronts are all gone and the buildings are now houses.

Hope Street, Crook. 5750

The Royal Hotel in Crook stood at the heart of the town, where Church Street, Commercial Street, Elliott Street and Hope Street, visible here, met. Stand on this spot today and you'll see much of Hope Street's buildings still standing. But as for the Royal Hotel, which operated for many years, a poor, modern imitation of the former public house stands in its place.

ROTTON ROW, CROOK

Rotten Row was an aptly named row of old cottages by the side of Crook Beck, occupied by workers of the nearby mill, some of whom are posing for this photograph. The small bridge is still there today, but the cottages are gone.

St Catherine's Church of England Church has been at the heart of Crook since 1841, off North Terrace and Church Street, and is still a thriving Christian community for the local population. This early painted postcard gives an idea of some of the surrounding landscape beyond the town, and the businesses on Mill Street.

Crook Market Place looking north. To the right is the Electric Palace, which has the distinction of being the oldest purpose-built cinema in northern England. It dates from 1910 and, while not in use as a cinema since the 1960s, it is hoped to restore it to this use once again.

The Northern Echo said of the Electric Palace's opening: "Mr Lowther JP, in a neat speech, declared the palace open, and said he hoped there would always be exhibited pictures which would be entertaining and elevating.

"The National Anthem was sung by the audience. The pictures were of the highest order, and g ave immense satisfaction."

ST. MARY'S AVENUE, CROOK

St. Mary's Avenue is a residential street of semi-detached houses north of Crook's town centre. It has a pleasant green area in the centre of the street, which the road loops around.

An atmospheric view along Front Street in Langley Park, complete with small businesses and their customers posing for the camera outside. At the end of the street, where it meets Logan Street, is the Langley Park Hotel, a small hostelry which still exists today as 'The Langley'.

While pavements were more substantial in this period, roads were still fairly primitive affairs with few automobiles using them. Note the horse and cart turning at the end of the scene.

An overview of Langley Park and its terraced rows of houses built to house workers at the village's mine, which can also be seen in the distance beyond the streets.

The village school, which was a filming location for the movie *Billy Elliott*, can be seen to the left of the houses in the centre of the picture.

Another view of Langley Park Colliery, which opened in 1873 and closed on 31 October 1975. It was created by the Consett Iron Company to work coal seams under the area, and transferred to the National Coal Board in 1947.

Named after nearby Eshwood Hall, this street in New Brancepeth has sadly been lost. It is typical of the streets and housing in many north eastern towns, where industrial activity such as mining brought thousands of new workers to the area.

Two historic views of Spennymoor's High Street. While the growth of industry around the town had seen a rise in employment and swelling of the town's population, poorer years were close by the time of these pictures. These scenes were typical of the early 20th century, with the local population and traders out in force, and horses used for carrying goods around town.

Another view of Spennymoor High Street from an elevated position. The absence of the Town Hall and its iconic clock tower dates this picture to before 1916, when the structure was opened on the right of the view.

In this view, the Town Hall has been constructed. Motor vehicles have also replaced the horses and carts so prevalent in previous pictures. If you stood in this position today, you will find that Dundas Street has cut through the buildings on either side of the High Street.

This early postcard is labelled Coulton Street in Low Spennymoor. A little investigation reveals that this is in fact Coulson Street. It still exists today, and the scene above, including the shop and buildings on the right, has been mostly cleared. The elegant old primary school building on the left still stands, on the junction with Vyners Close, but is now used as an auto tyre and exhaust centre.

Cheapside is at the eastern end of Spennymoor's High Street. It has always been an extension of the retail and commercial heart of the town. The picture is dated roughly by the presence of Gowland's Arcadia Grand Electric Hall, which opened in 1910 with seating for 1,000 people. A fire in 1929 led to it being rebuilt and renamed the Arcadia Cinema in 1931. Today it is a public house and restaurant.

Granville Terrace in the centre of Wheatley Hill seen in the early 1900s. The description on the postcard reads 'The Farm', and is likely to refer to Rock Farm, which is out of sight on the left of the scene and still present today. It is actually the oldest structure surviving in Wheatley Hill, dating to the 1500s.

The entrance to Wheatley Hill's cemetery on Cemetery Road. The Edwardian chapel of rest building on the right is now the Wheatley Hill Heritage Centre.

Wheatley Hill Colliery changed the face of the village. Pits searching for coal were begun in 1830, with the main shaft of what would become the Wheatley Hill and Thornley collieries sunk in 1869. The new mine transformed the village, bringing in a wave of miners to work the seams. A hundred years later, in 1969, the last workers clocked off and the mine was closed.

Another lost treasure of County Durham is the Empress Cinema in Willington. Opened in September 1927, it had an auditorium which could seat a thousand people and showed all of the popular pictures of the day. The grand building was closed in 1969 and has now been demolished. It once stood on Commercial Street (labelled High Street on this postcard), where the former railway station and bridge over the line can also be seen in this picture. These have also now been demolished.

July 22nd 1908 saw the unveiling of a memorial to Thomas Barton in Willington's St Stephen's churchyard by the mayor of Darlington, accompanied by a brass band.

Thomas was a miner at Brancepeth Colliery and, on the night of January 16th, 1908, he heard a cry for help on Railway Terrace in Willington. A fire was raging in a house, and a woman was screaming that her child was trapped upstairs. Showing incredibly bravery he entered the house and was inside when it collapsed. He was lucky to escape only with injuries, but sadly the child died.

Thomas Brown became a local hero, but his luck was up when he was killed by an underground collapse of stone in the mine only a month later.

Brandon Colliery Station in 1965, shortly after it had closed but before demolition. The pit after which it was named would close three years later. You'd be hard pressed to find any evidence of it today as the cutting in which it sat has now been filled in and a footpath runs along at the elevated level. The street named Station View is perhaps the best hint at its former location.

NORTH DURHAM

Front Street, Annfield Plain. (650)

A view of the thriving heart of Annfield Plain in northern County Durham. Visible are the underground public toilets in the middle of the road, which were closed in 1917 when a man fell down the stairs.

On the left is the Railway Hotel, and on the right the Queen's Head Hotel, and the now lost railway crossing at the end of the street.

Looking along New Front Street in Annfield Plain, close to the adjoining mining village of Catchgate. The large building at the centre of the picture is St. John's Methodist chapel, which existed until 1970.

Beamish Hall in the early 20th century, complete with croquet hoops on the neat lawn. Today this Grade II* listed building is a popular and stunning private hotel in large grounds. It was operated as a school briefly in the 1990s. The present building replaced an older manor in the 18th century, and many guests at the hotel have reported ghostly goings on in the rooms and hallways!

Famous the world over for its open air museum, Beamish is also a village in its own right. Previously known as Pit Hill, it lies just to the south east of the museum and consists of a few rows of houses and other amenities along the north side of the road.

This scene is the epitome of the rural County Durham village in days gone by. At a crossroads, the village of Castleside on the edge of what is now the Pennines Area of Natural Beauty, with the traditional signpost showing directions to Consett, Leadgate, Waskerley and Stanhope. Further on a horse and cart stand outside a village shop, and beyond is the Smelters Arms pub – both of which are now private houses.

The northern end of Front Street, which is Chester-le-Street's main commercial thoroughfare and has been for a long time. This view has changed somewhat since the picture was taken in the early 1920s. Most of the buildings have been replaced or altered. The Dun Cow Hotel building on the right still exists, now as three shops.

In the second picture, you can see the large Co-Operative Society building which was built in the 1930s, replacing the older buildings, including the one with the corner spire.

The Hermitage to the south west of Chester-le-Street was built around 1820 for the Featherstonhaugh family. It became a rehabilitation centre for Durham miners in 1944, and today the Grade II listed manor is once again in private hands, having been converted into luxury apartments.

The historic Lambton Arms coaching house on Front Street can be seen on the right here, shortly after it was remodelled in the early 1900s. It is still open today.

North End, Front Street, Chester-le-Street.

The north end of Front Street showing its junction with Picktree Lane on the left, and many early motorcars using the streets. How much quieter than today!

The large building on the right is Chester-le-Street Methodist Church. In the distance is the tall spire of St Mary & St Cuthbert's Church.

A wonderful aerial view of Chester-le-Street probably in the 1940s or 50s. The town's iconic Chester Burn railway viaduct of 11 arches, completed in 1868 and today carrying the East Coast Mainline between Durham and Newcastle. It dominates the town's market place below.

While Chester-le-Street is built on the small Chester Burn stream, the more significant River Wear passes just to the east of the town. These boaters are enjoying an outing on the river.

THE RIVER WEAR AT CHESTER-LE-STREET

A major event in Chester-le-Street for many years was the Shrove Tuesday football game held on Front Street, where those 'up-street' battled those 'down-street'. Teams could be any size, and rules were non-existent. The aim was to get the leather ball to one end or other of the street by any means possible.

The starting point was Lloyd's Bank, opposite the Lambton Arms, where the ball would be thrown from an upper window.

The local police outlawed the event from 1932, owing to the potential risk to life and property from the hundreds of players and spectators who descended on the town. In the first picture you can see windows boarded up, as owners tried to protect their property from the chaos of the game.

Some of the businesses on Front Street during the 1940s.

Ian Nairn said of Consett in his book *Nairn's County Durham*: "Consett is a steel town, and the works make a superb skyline all round north-western Durham, a smoking inferno balanced by the great swells of the hills." This description really comes alive when looking at this photograph of the town's iron works in full swing, with chimneys and smoke dominating the horizon. Look for this view today and you'll find it has all gone.

Blackhill to the west of Consett, known for its colliery and these sweeping views towards the Durham Dales – a typical contrast between industry and rural life so famous of this county.

Looking up Durham Road towards Blackhill. The walls on the left are the boundary of Benfield Hall, now a care home. The building on the corner on the right is now The Cricketers public house. The two people posing in the road are possibly the owners or tenants of this building.

Looking east across Blackhill with the Baptist Church dominant in the centre, and the rows of terraced houses on the horizon. The fields in the foreground, with bales of hay ready to be collected, are now the site of a housing estate.

Bustling Middle Street in Consett, and an amazing memory of life in the town's centre. In it people go about their daily life, young boys pose for the camera, nannies push prams, shops sell their wares, and faintly visible at the end of the street is the tower of Christ Church.

Middle Street still exists, but many of the buildings in this view are now gone, replaced by modern blocks. The Wesleyan Church visible half-way down the street on the right closed in 1968 and made way for a discount supermarket. This commercial heart of the town, like many across the North East, has struggled and is today home to closed businesses and shuttered buildings.

Front Street in Consett where it meets Middle Street (on the left). The view includes the lost Town Hall and water fountain on the corner, as well as the Empire Theatre further along which is still open today. The terraced houses further on have also been demolished and replaced by a modern pub. Early motor cars and many of the town's workers complete the scene from the 1940s.

On the edge of the northern Pennines, winters could sometimes be harsh, and none more so than that of early 1910. Here Rowley Station, south of Consett, is blanketed in snow and the train at the platform is blocked in. It would take an enormous effort to clear the track and allow it to continue its journey, with passengers forced to spend the night onboard or in the station house.

Plasworth is situated on the Great North Road, to the east of Sacriston. Today the village is split in two by the modern dual carriageway, and the Red Lion pub still exists. However, today it is much expanded and enlarged from this very early picture. Its position on this important roadway guaranteed regular trade, as it surely must today.

On the northern edge of Stanley, Station Road in Shield Row winds its way down to the heart of the small town, and its station. The people walking past these elegant houses look like they hav e a bit of a climb to negotiate!

STATION, SHIELD ROW.

Shield Row Station sat at the bottom of the hill where the railway line between Annfield Plain and Beamish. It opened in 1894 and was officially known as West Stanley Station. The green and cream wooden buildings were standard of many stations at the time, as was the footbridge.

In the first decade of the 1900s, Shield Row was the busiest station on the line, but competition from bus services saw a decline and in 1955 it closed, with good services lingering on until 1961. The site today is occupied by some garages, and the track bed now a cycle route.

Shield Row.

Shield Row looking up the steep incline of Gordon Terrace, and a poor horse dragging its cart uphill. Note the gas lamps, and the small shop at the left edge of the picture advertising Cadbury's Chocolate in its window – no doubt to the delight of the children gathered outside. Amazingly this building is still a corner shop today.

The centre of Shotley Bridge, where Front Street twists its way around the difficult terrain, and Burnmill Bank descends away to cross the River Derwent out of sight below. The interesting castellated house on the corner has now been demolished. It and the shops on the right have been replaced by modern, but tasteful, houses.

An overview of Shotley Bridge, which sits on the River Derwent between Consett and the Durham Dales. The town's larger church buildings are visible, and the terraced houses at Blackhill are on the horizon.

The beautiful River Derwent valley lies close to the heart of Shotley Bridge. The Sneep, sat in its natural bowl and bend in the river, is one of the most popular places, with unusual rock formations to see. It is full of folklore relating to the legend of King Arthur, who will supposedly be enthroned there once again.

The Anna S Proctor care home has existed in this building on Summerhill in Shotley Bridge since around the turn of the last century. It is named in honour of a local resident who spent much of her life invalided and, along with her sister who cared for her, set up a charity in 1891 to care for others in a similar situation. This building was purchased with the fund after she died in 1898, and named in her honour. Here staff pose outside the building in its early days. While the building lay empty for several years, it was once again opened as a care home in 1984.

It may seem a little macabre to produce a postcard about a disaster in which 165 people died, but this is just what has been done here. A multi-view card shows various scenes, including people waiting for news outside the West Stanley Colliery buildings.

The explosion occurred on February 16th, 1909, when coal dust and gas was ignited, although an exact cause was never determined and only recommendations could be made into improving the equipment and safety precautions at the site.

Coffins carrying men and boys who were victims of the West Stanley Colliery Disaster in 1909 process through Front Street in the town where thousands of the town's residents and fellow miners turn out to pay their respects. It was one of the darkest days in the region's history.

Young boys pose for the camera outside the elegant terraced houses along Station Road in Stanley. The houses are still present, but the horses and carts have long gone.

Following the West Stanley disaster in 1909 various measures were put in place to improve safety. This photograph shows the newly completed wheel and structures over the main shaft.

Passengers board a train at Lanchester Station on the Lanchester Branch of the North Eastern Railway - a line constructed to ease transport the product of nearby ironworks to Teesside. Passenger services were also provided, but little used and the station closed to all but occasional services in 1939, and to goods trains in 1965. The old station house is now a holiday cottage.

EAST DURHAM & THE COAST

Castle Eden is now somewhat bypassed by most people since the A19 motorway opened in the 1970s and the namesake brewery closed. The quiet little village is home to a popular golf club, cricket club and a couple of inns.

St. James' church is located close to the castle itself, to the east of the village. It was built in 1764 on the site of an older chapel, but today is not used for regular services.

The heart of Castle Eden village looking along the road leading to the church and castle, which in reality is no more than a grand manor house dating from the 1760s. These traditional cottages date from a similar period, once housing workers from the castle and nearby farms. They still stand today.

Not to be confused with the main Coxhoe railway station, Coxhoe Bridge was a second halt which existed on the Ferryhill to Hartlepool branch line to the south of the town. Its two platforms were staggered either side of the road bridge, which today is the busy A177. The station's proximity to local mine pits meant it was used in the carriage of goods as well as passengers.

Nothing in this picture remains today except the road. The former railway line is a popular walkway.

Cornforth Lane leads into Coxhoe from the direction of Cornforth and Ferryhill to the south west. These semi-detached houses, seen looking towards the Coxhoe Primary School at the edge of the town, were for slightly more affluent residents compared to the tightly packed terraces at the centre of the town.

Easington Colliery Primary School on Seaside Lane at the heart of the town. The grand Victorian buildings opened in the late 1800s and saw many of the town's children educated. However, since 1997 the buildings, which are Grade II listed, have been empty and derelict awaiting a decision on their future.

The ancient village of Easington is surrounded by the more modern mining town of Easington Colliery. At the heart of the old town is Low Row, where traditional cottages, a chapel and the Kings Head pub lie.

At the end of its life as a pub, the King's Head suffered a devastating fire. However, developers have now restored this building and turned it into residential dwellings. The King's Head title still adorns the building, however.

An incredibly rare and evocative image of the interior of Horden's Working Men's Social Club showing bartenders and patrons in the early 1900s.

At the heart of social life outside the workplace, most Durham towns and villages had a similar club which served local working men with affordable drinks, and a place to relax and play pub games.

HORDEN CLUB BEFORE THE FIRE.

HORDEN CLUB AFTER THE FIRE.

Horden Club suffered a devastating fire in 1910, caused by unrest among the village's workers. These pictures show the building before and after the fire.

Owing to the popularity of such an establishment, it was rebuilt and went on to serve the village for many years, becoming one of County Durham's most famous working men's clubs. It closed in the 1990s and has now been demolished.

Looking up Broadway in the centre of Houghton le Spring towards the White Lion Hotel, whose building dated from around 1827. In its early days petty court sessions were held here, until the nearby police station was built.

Today the White Lion still exists on this spot, but the building itself was rebuilt in a less attractive style in the mid-1960s, along with the adjoining shopping parade.

Remarkably this narrow stretch of pubic houses, and even The Victoria public house on the right, still exist on Church Street in Murton. Further along the road today you'll find the large Dalton Park Outlet shopping centre.

Looking down what was then Railway Street in Seaham, heading towards the harbour. Today this stretch is known as Castlereagh Road and, of the grand buildings visible on the left, only the central one with the white window lintels, and some of those beyond it, still stand.

The opposite side of the road, on the right of the picture, was once the railway line leading into Seaham Harbour Station. It is now a path, with the station having been demolished in 1971.

An historic view of Seaham Harbour's docks where coal from the Durham minefields was loaded onto ships for many years. The docks remain today, but the scene here is now full of smaller pleasure craft instead of large colliers.

FRONT STREET, WINGATE. 2147.

Front Street is Wingate's main commercial road where shops and other businesses carried out their trade. As with many County Durham towns, there has been a significant decline in villages like Wingate since the coal mines were closed in the 1980s, and Front Street today is a much quieter place.

Founded in 1838, Holy Trinity Church was built shortly after the first pits were sunk in this north-east County Durham mining village. Along with the nearby Methodist Church, it served the spiritual needs of the many workers and their families who came to live here.

Looking across the railway line leading to one of Wingate's two former railway stations. Both are now long gone, along with the line and most of the buildings and businesses visible in this picture.

SOUTH DURHAM

With grand buildings, businesses and homes on all sides, and a church on an island in the middle, Bishop Auckland's Market Place is one of the finest in the region. This lovely view shows some of the traders to be found here, including Doggarts – the department store with chains across the region, but with their home in Auckland House on the Market Place in Bishop Auckland. It remained here until the business closed in 1980.

A fine example of an early motor bus with driver and passengers posing outside shops in Bishop Auckland.

The foundation stone of the Wesleyan Church in Bishop Auckland was laid in 1912 and this Grade II listed building features a stained glass window memorial for World War I. The church closed in 1993 and was transformed into the Four Clocks Centre in 2002, offering all kinds of support to local residents and charities. South Road itself was later renamed Newgate Street.

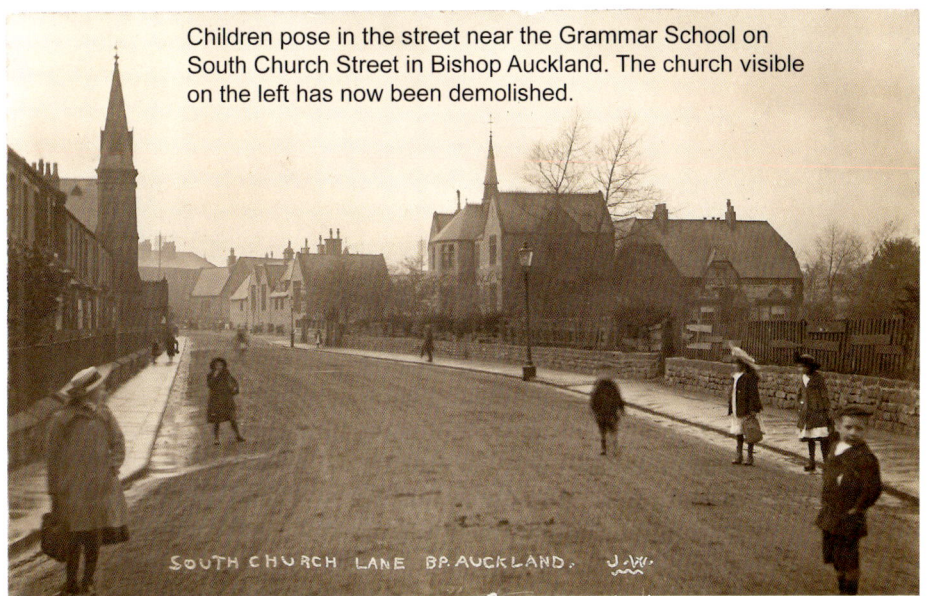

Children pose in the street near the Grammar School on South Church Street in Bishop Auckland. The church visible on the left has now been demolished.

Bishop Auckland's Primitive Methodist Chapel on Cockton Hill Road. It still stands, now opposite the hospital, and is an important part of the town's Christian history. The building dates from 1903 and is Grade II listed.

Looking down Cockton Hill Road. The spires of its two churches are prominent – the Baptist Church on the left, and the Primitive Methodist Chapel on the right. Both still stand, as do the elegant terraced houses on this busy road which once formed the Roman road named Dere Street.

Some readers may remember the businesses visible here in this 1950s view of Bishop Auckland's main shopping thoroughfare, Newgate Street. Some of the buildings still stand, and others have been altered or replaced.

Standing in Etherley Lane on the western edge of Bishop Auckland today, it's hard to believe it was once this quiet country lane. It is now a very busy road, and the open fields largely replaced by modern housing.

Another view of Newgate Street in 1912 with its thriving businesses and local residents going about their business.

A photograph taken from the west overlooking Dam Head and River Wear towards the Newton Cap Viaduct and road bridge leading into Bishop Auckland from Toronto. The town's rugby club occupies the land in the centre of the picture.

Escomb is unique in County Durham, and in much of Britain for that matter. Here you'll find a complete, unaltered Saxon church built around 675AD. By the time of this picture recent works to secure and restore the building and its roof had been undertaken, following centuries of neglect and without a resident vicar. Today it is still in regular use, and a major place of Christian pilgrimage and tourist attraction.

These two tourist postcards show Auckland Castle and its entrance, which are perhaps the most famous landmarks in this County Durham town. Between 1832 and 2012 this was the home of the Bishop of Durham – historically the famous Prince Bishops – and staff. There has actually been a castle on the site since the 12th century, and today's building is Grade I listed. While it still houses offices for the Diocese of Durham, it has been turned into a tourist attraction.

The Grade I listed Newton Cap Bridge in the foreground, and Newton Gap Viaduct in the background, crossing the River Wear into Bishop Auckland. The Grade II listed viaduct was built in 1857 to carry the railway into the town, but was turned into a road bridge in 1995 in order to relieve the original stone bridge which has origins in the 14th century.

Bishop Auckland's Market Place with traders and stalls in place. In the distance are the gates at the entrance to Auckland Castle, and in the centre are St Anne's Church and Bishop Auckland Town Hall.

Auckland Castle and its gardens, which have recently been restored and opened to the public as part of the town's revival.

The Gothic gates and clock tower at the entrance to Auckland Castle off Bishop Auckland's Market Place. Built in 1760 by Sir Thomas Robinson of Rokeby, the grand entrance was awarded Grade I listed status in 1952.

Situated on the eastern edge of Ferryhill at the bottom of Lough Bank, its station existed from 1835 until 1967. It was recommended to close by the Beeching Cuts, but local opposition meant it had a reprieve for a couple of years, gradually losing passenger service, and then being gutted by a fire.

Today some of the buildings in this view still exist, including the Eldon Arms pub directly ahead. The railway bridge carries the road over the line, which is still there, but nothing remains of the station itself.

The graceful Eldon Terrace opposite Ferryhill station. Today these houses still exist, but have lost their uniformity to a mixture of remodelled windows and various types of cladding. Newer houses have been built opposite, blocking the view of the railway line which in this shot shows a complicated arrange of signals and telegraph poles.

Like most small towns, Ferryhill had its own cinema. The Gaiety Electric Theatre operated from 1912 until 1967 on Main Street. The building was demolished in 1994.

A more compact Ferryhill than today, where the busy Darlington Road crosses Church Lane and Merrington Road. Ahead is the Black Bull, which still exists. In this photo you can just make out the titles, and the fact it offers billiards. Beyond it are a clothing store, fruiterer and a shop advertising Hunters Tea. The sign of the Red Lion is just visible – a pub which has since been lost.

Just over today's Ferryhill Cut, which carries the A167 through the town largely out of sight, this is Merrington Road and the Dean Bank School on the left. Opposite is the Dean Bank Miners Institute, part of which still stands, albeit modified. Beyond are the rows of terraced houses which used to be home to miners working at the Dean and Chapter Colliery.

Dean and Chapter Colliery was Ferryhill's coal mine, situated to the north west of the town centre. Construction started in 1902, and it finally closed on 3rd December 1968. In this view the famous Ferryhill Cut can be seen, taking the road through the centre of the town. It was constructed in 1923 and today is the busy A167 between Darlington and Durham.

Looking up Darlington Road towards the centre of Ferryhill. The Black Bull is visible at the top of the hill, and the terraces on the right are home to many small businesses and traders. With the Ferryhill Cut opening in the 1920s, this main thoroughfare – once the A1 – became much quieter.

Another view of the Dean Bank Miners Institute on Merrington Road. The Dean Bank area sprang up with the construction of the nearby colliery, housing thousands of workers, and the Institute was a place for those men and boys to go for support. Today the building is run as the Dean Bank and Ferryhill Literary Institute, offering community support and education for local residents.

The Hardwick Arms is a Grade II listed building in the centre of Sedgefield, occupying a prominent position overlooking the High Street and Church View. The present building dates from the early 19th Century and has an original archway to allow carriages through to the stable yard.

The labelled "tenement" on this postcard is not necessarily to indicate squalid housing, but the local name for this row of old cottages behind the church in Sedgefield. They were later renamed Rectory Row, although many of buildings in the area have been demolished. The building on the right still exists, and has been modernised.

Sedgefield High Street with the imposing tower of St Edmund's Parish Church in its raised churchyard at the centre of the village.

Looking along Darlington Road in Sadberge, a couple of miles to the east of Darlington. The wall on the left marks the edge of the churchyard of St Andrew's, while the shop ahead is advertising Fry's Chocolate and Capstan Cigarettes.

Once the main road between Stockton and Darlington, Sadberge was bypassed by the new A66 motorway in the 1970s.

Main Street in Shildon with two of the town's main churches. Ahead is St John's Parish Church, while on the right is Shildon Methodist Church's original building. This has now been demolished and replaced by a modern and much smaller brick building. Between the two churches is the York City and County Banking Company building, which is today a branch of HSBC.

A dramatic view along the long stretch of terraced houses forming Main Street in Shildon. Note one of the houses on the right seems to be operating as a library.

The view is little changed today, save for some of the terraces having been replaced by modern houses, and the road which is now much busier.

A group of Shildon ladies in various uniforms pose to celebrate the coronation of King George V in 1911.

A colour postcard view looking along Church Street in Shildon and the various small shops and businesses that were in operation in the early 20th century. Today, this street is much as it was, however the buildings on the left in this particular view have been replaced by a 1960s block of shops. The grander building at the back of the scene still stands, and is home to a coffee shop today.

Another photographic view of St John's Church and the York City and County Bank on Main Street in Shildon. The buildings on the left have been replaced or altered and the wide pavement with these newly planted trees has become off street parking.

An elevated view of Main Street in Shildon taken from the tower of St John's Church. The old Methodist Church building is on the left, and the town's terraces and works are in the distance. Note the amount of smoke emanating from all the chimneys.

Looking up Church Street. The Red Lion Hotel is just visible half-way up on the left, on the corner of Association Street. This still exists today as a public house, but the building's upper levels have been removed. It's still possible to see the ornate brick work on the buildings on the right, which are now houses.

The grand vicarage standing just behind St John's Church in central Shildon.

 The original Trimdon Village as it looked before it expanded to the south when modern housing was built. This is looking along Front Street, where the road is still rough and horses are the main form of transport. The building with the sign on the left is the Fox and Hounds pub, which still operates today. The corner of St Mary Magdalene Church, which dates from the Norman period, is visible on the right.

A view of the station in the colliery village of Trimdon Station, taken around 1905 and showing the station buildings, tracks and passengers waiting on the platform. This station served the colliery between 1834 and 1964 and is now completely demolished, as is the line,

Prospect Terrace in Trimdon Station, now known as Prospect Place. This scene includes some of the older houses and the old Primitive Methodist Chapel, all of which have been demolished. A smaller, modern Methodist church replaced this building, and modern houses replaced the terraces. The taller building farthest from the camera still exists, albeit in a poor condition.

Front Street in Trimdon Grange around 1915. This was a busy place with all manner of businesses, shops, houses and places of entertainment and worship. The railway line crossed the road behind the camera. By the 1960s this area had declined considerably, and the buildings here were demolished in the 1970s leaving this road, now known as Salters Lane, with large open areas of grass and no sign of its former life.

Much more than just an old bridge, this was in fact the first cast iron bridged to be used on a railway, and crossed the River Gaunless in West Auckland between 1823 and 1901. It was designed by George Stephenson and built by John and Isaac Burrell. Today the stone plinths are still visible, next to Oakley Green, and the bridge itself is preserved at the Locomotion Museum in Shildon.

The eastern end of Front Street and the Green in West Auckland. This row of buildings still mostly stand, with the taller building at the right edge of the picture now under the modern Station Road. Ian Nairn described West Auckland's Green as 'a great void'.

Darlington Road leading in to West Auckland. Today it is the A68 and most of the blocks of terraced houses seen here have been replaced by newer houses. The open area opposite houses a large factory, as well as West Auckland Football Club's ground.

An old stone bridge carrying the road over the River Gaunless in West Auckland, now replaced by a modern structure.

Bridge, West Auckland.

Children gather on The Green in High Coniscliffe, one of the most southerly villages in County Durham, situated on the north bank of the River Tees, opposite North Yorkshire. The village's name is derived from *King's Cliff*, after the ridge of limestone above the river near the ancient St Edwin's church.

Darlington doesn't have a High Street, but instead has High Row – a multi-level main thoroughfare in the centre of the town with an terrace of tall, elegant buildings housing shops and banks overlooking the Town Hall and covered market place below.

County Durham's place in the world is surely defined by the introduction of the world's first public steam-powered railway, which ran between Shildon, Darlington and Stockton from 1825. The Stockton & Darlington Railway paved the way for a revolution in travel and the transportation in goods which would make the world a smaller place.

These two pictures celebrate the scenes at the opening of the railway in September 1825 as crowds gather to watch Locomotion No. 1 pass the Skerne Bridge in Darlington. The second shows the same train on the platform at Darlington's Bank Top station, where it was preserved for many years before being moved to the museum at North Road.

A busy scene along Bondgate in Darlington around 1920, with one of the town's trams working its way up the bank from High Row in the centre of the town.

WEST DURHAM & TEESDALE

The ruins of Egglestone Abbey lie in a secluded location a couple of miles south east of Barnard Castle. Nearby a stone toll bridge built in 1773 crosses the River Tees. This view of the bridge in the early days of motor vehicles shows a wonderful scene where tolls are being taken.

Today it's still possible to cross the Abbey Bridge, but the toll booths are long gone, with only their circular foundations visible on the southern side.

The impressive French-style Bowes Museum resembles a huge country mansion. Yet the building, on the outskirts of Barnard Castle, was never a home and was purpose-built as an art gallery by John Bowes and his wife Joséphine Benoîte Coffin-Chevallier. It opened in 1892, after both had died, and is seen here around 40 years later.

Today it houses a hugely important collection of art, with hundreds of paintings and sculptures on display by many renowned artists.

Never considered an architectural gem, Streatlam Castle was nevertheless one of the three homes of the Bowes-Lyon family, who were ancestors of Queen Elizabeth The Queen Mother, and those responsible for the Bowes Museum.

Built on the site of an older castle, the large mansion sat a few miles north east of Barnard Castle, off the present-day A688. By the 1940s its last inhabitant had moved on and many of its contents were quickly recovered before the Army was allowed to blow the building up as demolition practice in 1959. Today only the entrance lodges remain, guarding the large parkland which were once the castle's grounds. Many of the castle's rescued artwork and other items are on display at Glamis Castle in Scotland.

A number of war memorials now exist in Barnard Castle. This, commemorating the Boer War of 1859-1902, was the earliest and still stands on Galgate, as do the shops behind. It was unveiled in 1905 by Colonel V Grimshaw of the third Battalion Durham Light Infantry. Since then a memorial garden has been built around it.

A fantastic view over the rooftops of central Barnard Castle looking along Newgate towards the Bowes Museum which rises on the horizon. Beyond it is Barnard Castle School, and in the foreground is the Primitive Methodist Chapel on Newgate which stood between 1887 and 1992 and is now the site of a car park. Its stained glass window was rescued and inserted into Barnard Castle Methodist Church.

An atmospheric scene looking up the River Tees towards the imposing ruins of Barnard Castle on its craggy outcrop. The stone fortification was built in the 12th century and gave the town its name.

Galgate in Barnard Castle then, as now, has lovely tree-lined islands down the centre of the road. Many of the elegant houses along this stretch of road are built of local stone and would have been lived in by the more wealthy residents of the town.

Dating from Norman times, the church of St Thomas in Stanhope was already old by the time this photograph was taken. The Grade II* listed building stands overlooking the Market Square and features a square tower and beautiful stained glass windows. It is the heart of one of the largest parishes in England, and traditionally was rich from the tithes of workers at the prosperous local lead mines.

The River Wear meanders by to the south of the village of Stanhope. Here is a view along the river walkway, with the now-lost suspension bridge visible in the background.

This is a scene on Main Street in Stanhope which has altered somewhat today. While the Phoenix Hotel building on the left still survives, now as The Bonny Moorhen pub, the building ahead occupied by P. Daley as a chemist and grocer, has been lost. The road here is now much wider as the busy A689. Many of the buildings on the left still stand, occupied by modern businesses in this Weardale village.

Stanhope Castle is a beautiful 18th-Century manor complex on the Market Place at the heart of Stanhope. It is thought to stand on the site of an older castle, and looks very imposing today, even if it's not as old as it makes out.

Set among extensive grounds, this scene shows two ladies posing at the entrance. They are likely to be members of one of the families who leased the castle between 1866 and when it was turned into a school for boys in 1941.

Main Street is also known as Front Street in Stanhope. This view is looking towards the Market Place, Castle and church with the various small businesses and pubs in the historic buildings on the right.

Cotherstone is in the most westerly parish of County Durham, which extends to the Cumbrian border. This pretty old village was, in fact, part of the North Riding of Yorkshire until 1974 when the boundaries changed. Built around the agricultural industries, Cotherstone today is an area of outstanding natural beauty.

This vies is looking west along the main road through the village. The Red Lion pub is visible beyond the horse and cart.

One of the most iconic landmarks of County Durham is High Force waterfall on the River Tees a few miles upstream from Middleton-in-Teesdale. Long a draw for tourists and visitors, the falls drop around 70 feet. During times of high rainfall the flow can be quite dramatic, and in colder spells the falls have been known to freeze.

HIGH FORCE, Middleton-in-Teesdale.

A selection of photographic scenes of Middleton-in-Teesdale from the early 1900s. Owing to the area's natural beauty, it has long drawn visitors. The scenes on show here highlight some of the attractions, including hotels, bridges over the Tees, High Force Waterfall, and the Horse Market in the centre of the town.

Middleton-in-Teesdale's Market Place complete with a cart parked in the road. This view today can be quite busy with cars parked either side of the road and visitors enjoying the village. The Teesdale Hotel is on the right with its sign hanging outside. Then, as today, this is a popular place to stay or enjoy refreshments.

A view of Horse Market, which is around the corner from the Market Place and, as the name suggests, was historically the place where horses were bought and sold. Chapel Row is the smaller road running alongside Horse Market and is named after the Methodist Chapel built here.

Tow Law's Primitive Methodist Chapel. Built in 1846, it provided for the Christian congregations in the village alongside churches of other denominations, until it was closed and demolished in 1965 when the ground became unstable. It was located on Dan's Castle, opposite the cemetery. The terraces on either side still exist in the most part.

Quite a crowd awaits this Class V3 steam locomotive as it pulls into the old station at Middleton in Teesdale, suggesting a special occasion or VIP guest on board.

This station was the end of the line from Barnard Castle, operating between 1868 and 30 November 1964. Some remnants of it still exist at its former location on a caravan park a mile south of the village.

DURHAM CITY

View from the Railway Station.   Durham.

A typical postcard view of Durham taken from the railway station, intended to entice and delight tourists to the city, or thinking of visiting the city, by the impressive vista which awaits them.

The medieval Elvet Bridge in Durham with its 'old houses', which incidentally are still standing today. The bridge was built in the 12th century to link the centre of Durham with the expanded Elvet area on the opposite bank of the river.

DURHAM; IN WINTER

The River Wear in Durham has been known to freeze over on occasion. This Auty Series postcard shows such an occasion around 1910 when locals ventured onto the ice to skate and play games.

The majestic view of Durham Cathedral from the river below is always an impressive sight.

Framwellgate Bridge is one of two medieval, Grade I listed bridges in Durham. The other is Elvet Bridge. It has two main arches and replaced an older structure, and was itself widened in the 19th century to the structure we see today, and in this early 1900s picture with the cathedral and castle as a backdrop.

Durham Cathedral.

A lovely painting of some of Durham's older, now lost medieval houses and the central tower of Durham Cathedral.

Durham Cathedral and River Wear.

This serene scene is looking up Bow Lane towards the west end of Durham Cathedral. The building on the left is known as Kingsgate, which is the original name for this narrow street.

Durham City in the early 20th century. This view over the rooftops really gives a sense of how compact the city is, and the amount of buildings that existed from the medieval period until much was cleared for modern developments in recent decades. The cathedral and castle are the crowning features of the city, visible for miles around, as intended.

Durham Castle has to be the finest, most unique student accommodation anywhere in the world. Dating from the Norman period, like the present cathedral, it was occupied in its original purpose as a fortification and home of the Bishop of Durham until 1837 when University College, Durham took it over.

The mound of the original motte and bailey castle can be seen under the present-day stone keep, visible in this picture.

Opened in October 1915, as this postcard says, the Durham Miners' Hall is on Redhills Lane. In fact, today it is known as Redhills. It is the headquarters of the Durham Miners' Association and houses the ornate Pitman's Parliament room where large gatherings were held. Today the building and Association are seeking a new purpose for the building as an cultural, heritage and education centre.

Another view of Elvet Bridge looking south from near where New Elvet Bridge stands today, on the city side of the river. Boats at the Boat Club can be seen on the right.

Prebends Bridge is the third of the old stone crossings of the River Wear in Durham, however this one is much younger, dating from the 1770s. It was built as a private bridge for the Dean and Chapter of Durham, coming ashore near the Westgate and southern side of the cathedral. Today it is only open to foot and cycle traffic.

The serene and peaceful cloisters at the heart of Durham Cathedral. Still a focal point for the building today, long after its monks left, they now form part of the visitor experience away from the main building.

Prebends Bridge and the River Wear during one of the great freezes. A daring crowd has gathered on the ice to pose for this picture.

The main nave of Durham Cathedral. This colossal space rises 73 feet to the ribbed and vaulted ceiling, while the combined length of the interior is almost 470 feet. It was completed in 1135.

An idyllic view towards Durham and its towering cathedral from Mount Joy to the south of the city, where hay bales have been prepared. Mount Joy today is part of the sprawling Durham University campus and no longer as much part of the agricultural landscape.

Durham Grammar School on Quarryheads Lane on the west bank of the River. Known today simply as Durham School it has a range of historic and very grand buildings, many listed, which provide for students and staff, as well as playing fields.

Not to be confused with the Redhills Miner's Hall, this is the original building used for the purpose. It is on North Road and was opened in 1876 with this grand clock tower. The Durham Miners moved to the Redhills site in 1915 and this building was used for a range of other purposes. Today it is a pub.

One of them most desirable locations in Durham is Queen Street, approaching Palace Green, the cathedral and castle. This old medieval house still stands and is in private hands, with original beams and floors extending outwards at each level.

The reason for Durham City's existence is the cathedral, built as a shrine to St Cuthbert after monks travelled around with is body after being forced to flee from Lindisfarne. The present Durham Cathedral was begun on the site of an older church in 1093 and is considered one of the finest Norman buildings in existence.

One of the narrow wooded lanes which traverse the banks of the River Wear in the western part of Durham and gives the city such appeal to visitors.

The lecture rooms and buildings on Palace Green outside the cathedral. Today they house the Museum of Archaeology as well as a Durham University library and Department of Music. The buildings to the left were part of the original Durham School from 1661 to 1844.

Narrow and twisting Silver Street which links Durham's Market Place to Framwellgate Bridge and beyond. It has always been a place of commerce, with small shops and traders just like today.

After Palace Green with the cathedral and castle, Durham's other focal point is the Market Place. This wide open space is surrounded with tall, grand buildings dating mostly from the Victorian era including St Nicholas' Church, the Town Hall and the Market Hall, plus the statue of the 3rd Marquess of Londonderry on his horse. Some are older, and some have been replaced by more modern buildings.

The Durham Light Infantry, or DLI, have always had a proud association with their home county. Here they are performing their Returning from Route march for onlookers after coming home from duty.

An early coloured postcard view of Elvet Bridge and Durham City.

Construction of Durham Gaol and House of Correction began in July 1809 thanks to a £2,000 gift from Bishop Barrington Shute. It was to replace the two older, cramped jails that existed in the city which were considered to be unfit for purpose.

The Georgian buildings which formed the new prison, in the Elvet part of the city, are among the most interesting and well-known of any prison in the country, thanks to their architecture, location and some of the famous prisoners who have been housed here. These include the Kray Twins, Rose West, Myra Hindley and Frankie Fraser. Today these buildings are the front of a large, modern complex known as HMP Durham. Another prison, HMP Frankland, was built to the north of the city in 1983.

An early picture of Durham's Elvet Methodist Church with its tall spire. It was built on Old Elvet in 1903 with seating for 746 people inside. It replaced an older Wesleyan chapel nearby, and it is still open today.

HOCKEY SENIORS 1907.

ST. HILD'S TENNIS TEAM. 1907.

Two wonderful memories of Durham University's sporting history, with the Hockey Seniors team and tennis team of St Hild and St Bede College, both in 1907. The clothing was somewhat more modest and restrictive compared to today.

A postcard featuring Durham Cathedral and its commanding position. It also features the Bishop of Durham of the time, Handley Moule. He presided from September 1901 until his death in 1920. He had previously been Honorary Chaplain to Queen Victoria until her death in 1901.

Durham Market Place and its largely Victorian buildings seen in the early 1900s. St Nicholas' Church, known locally as St Nic's, is one of the best known in the city. The present building replaced an older church in 1857.

The statue of Charles William Vane Tempest, the 3rd Marquess of Londonderry which was unveiled on this spot in Durham's Market Place in 1861. Depicted in his early life as a soldier, Tempest went on to own many of County Durham's mines and set about implementing better conditions for workers. He also had Seaham Harbour constructed to improve trade.

An important part of the role of Durham Cathedral in its early years was as a place of sanctuary for those who may have fallen foul of the law.

The Sanctuary Knocker was placed on the main northern door. Anyone who had committed a grave offence, such as murder or escape from prison, could knock on the door and receive 37 days of sanctuary in order to reconcile with their enemies or try to escape. They would wear a special robe while in sanctuary, adorned with St Cuthbert's Cross. This practice ended in 1624 and the original knocker is now in the cathedral's collection, while the present one is a replica.

Durham in 1745.   Auty Series, G.H., W.B., No. 670.

A lovely old drawing of Durham as it would have looked in 1745, before cameras could record pictures in detail. It shows, with some artistic license, the hilltop prominence of the city with its cathedral and castle atop. The original Prebends Bridge and Framwellgate Bridge span the river, and some of the more prominent churches can be seen, like St Cuthbert's in Elvet and St Giles in Gilesgate. The agricultural areas all around Durham would be lost to an expansion of the city's housing and university over the coming century.

Another atmospheric early 20th century view of Durham looking down from a high vantage point in Gilesgate. In the foreground is Elvet, while the castle and cathedral are silhouetted on the skyline. The many chimneys belching smoke show what the air quality must have been like in Durham until clean air acts came into force.

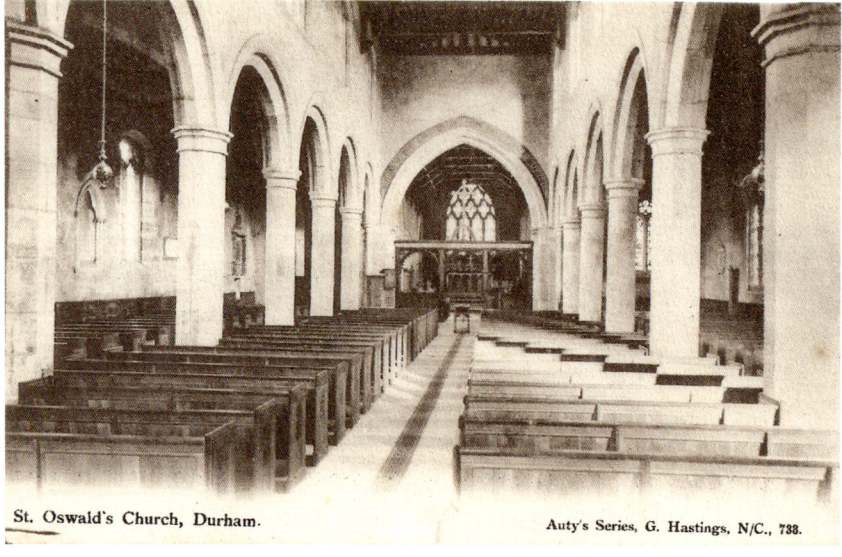

The interior of the historic St Oswald's Parish Church, one of the oldest Durham, built in the 12th century and rebuilt in 1834. It is Grade II* listed and much of the interior is original. You'll find it on Church Street, with the River Wear to its rear.

The corner of Pimlico and Grove Street where a horse and cart waits outside the corner building with its ornate plaque. Today this plaque has been replaced by a window, and since 1985 the building has part of Durham School's Pimlico House.

Finchale Priory has been in ruins since the 1530s Dissolution of the Monasteries. It lies in a lovely, secluded meander of the River Wear around 5 miles north east of Durham. The priory was founded in 1196 as an outpost of Durham Cathedral, where monks could go for rest. Today Finchale Priory is a Grade I listed English Heritage attraction, and much of the grounds are taken up by a holiday park.

Ramshackle buildings along South Street, presumably not long before they were cleared. The Curtain was the southern part of the street, below St Margaret's Church, and is now made up of luxury flats and student accommodation. It's interesting to see the fascinating array of posters and adverts on the building wall.

The original Durham County Hospital off North Road, near Durham Railway Station. It is a grand Elizabethan style building which opened in 1853 and finally closed, after several periods of expansion, in 2010. Since then the building has been reinvented at student accommodation known as Rushford Court.

Durham Castle's Great Hall is one of the largest examples in Britain, dating from the 13th century. Today it is the dining hall for this unique halls of residence, and still retains formal dining by students twice per week. The scribblings on this postcard indicate it may have been sent by a former pupil resident here.

Much of the stone used in the construction of Durham Castle was cut from the cliffs below and hauled up. Its towering position was meant to act as a formidable deterrent to any foes, particularly those from Scotland. Later the castle was entrusted to the Bishops of Durham to exercise royal authority on behalf of the king.

The ornate domed structure in Durham Market Place was the pant. It featured a statue of Neptune on top, and replaced an older example in 1863. As the name suggests, this strange structure was a public source of drinking water. It was removed in 1923.

Looking like a modern photograph, this coloured postcard shows Elvet Bridge in the early 20th century and its clear gradient as it descends from the Durham side to the Elvet side.

Durham Gilesgate Station was an early passenger terminus on the Newcastle & Darlington Junction Railway between 1844-1857, and predates the present-day railway station. It was not a viable long-term station since it was on a branch line.

Following its closure to passengers, this elegant station would then spend the next 109 years as a goods yard, which is evident in this picture. Today Gilesgate Station is a hotel.

Acknowledgements

This book on County Durham and its heritage has been a joy to put together with the continued support and help of my friend and publisher Matt Falcus. As ever Matt's encouragement, patience and faith in my abilities to plough ahead with this and other publications has enabled and empowered me to bring to fruition my passion for my postcard collection to be viewed and enjoyed by a much wider audience than just my family and friends.

Forgive this extensive acknowledgement page. However, in the surreal times we are enduring at the time of writing with a global pandemic and lockdowns, one comes to appreciate just how valuable family and friends are.

I wish to acknowledge those who have throughout my life been so loving, caring and supportive of all my hard work, passion and love for postcard collecting from 1966 onwards and as such I feel no embarrassment or offer any apology to the reader in listing so many as space permits, as they have never let me down these last 54 years.

My family as always are totally supportive and eagerly await whichever project I am working upon to come to fruition. As such I am blessed to have so many loving cousins, nephews and nieces, who have always been solidly behind all my endeavours.

Especially close are my brother Hamed, wife Karen and my loving niece Sofia, my caring, loving and supportive sister Shahadh and nieces Aysha and Fazia, and nephew Ahmed, his wife Lyndsey and son, young Musa. My sister in law Massurat and nephew Khurram plus his lovely wife Maria are some of my most virulent fans. My very loving nephew & "adopted" son Rizwan (Rizzy), his wife and also my niece Moqaddus and son young Rohaan are all always eager to learn of my latest project and fully back my endeavours, whatever I have may have embarked upon, as does my beautiful and very loving niece Jackie and her husband Khoolas and daughter Heidi living in Cyprus.

Other close family I must mention for their utmost support and encouragement are cousins Robina and Asghar's family, Adil, Shakeel, Hasaan and wife Javairia and my very supportive and loving nephew and friend Rahfe Rahim. My late aunt Naseem and Un. Anwars family, Saleem, Rubila and Sameena Chohan. My very closest of cousins and friend Ejaz Hassan, ever since he was a teenager, has been one of my longest and most loyal within the family together with other cousins such as Shahbaz and Imtiaz (Bobby) in Leicester and Baji Zehra and Bhai Ikram and family in Bristol.

Yet another of my adoring nieces is Sarah, her husband Azim and Son Sami plus cousin Gulshan and husband Raza and nephew Zain and niece Ummay, plus nephew Tayub in Manchester who all are never failing in their love for my books and eagerly await every new project that I am working on, as do my London sister Gurmesh (Carol) and all the loving Shina family. Other family include my very intellectual cousin Lydia Noor and her equally intelligent husband Norman in Pocklington plus sons William and George. Last but not least are cousin Vanda and John Sherwood in Acklam.

I would like to thank my wonderful extended family and friends in Pakistan, chief amongst them are my cousins Ruccka Rais and Bano, nephews Naeem and his family, Noor and Zawar and nieces Maynah and Kinza in Lahore. Last but not least are Nephews Azam and niece Shmyla, Asim and niece Amara in Gujranwala.

Also in Gujranwala are many close friends but the most ardent amongst them are, Abu Bakr (AB) and Umer (Bubbaloo) plus Zain and Amir. In Nowsherra Virkan my friends include Usman Saeed, Ahsan Virk and Faisal of Al Baik plus cousin Riaz, niece Rabia & husband Amar and nephew Arslaan who are all very happy recipients of my books.

Here in the UK as well all around the globe are many of my close friends who still look out for a postcard to add to my collection at fairs, bazaars and the odd shop. Foremost amongst them are Jazz and Moni Gill. Other close friends in London are Layla Hitchens, Lulu and Peter Vanvacass. In Leicester are David and Julie, and in Middlesbrough are George and Barbara, the lads from my cards group and my very, very close friend and fellow local author, Paul Stephenson.

My dearest friend Catherine Brown with children Rosa and Tyler. Catherine (Cathy) has been supportive of my postcard collecting ever since our first meeting in September 1968. Other long-standing, attentive, loyal friends going back to 1969 are Mary and Mike Day who to this day continue to look out for Teesside cards for me as do my dearest of friends David and Sandy Smith who now reside in Perth, Western Australia but are originally from Middlesbrough.

Others in Western Australia are my "Aussie Brother" Glenn Hankinson, his Lovely wife Olivia and fabulous boys, Preston and Brody, not forgetting my "Aussie Mum" Doris and late Keith (Dada) Hankinson and all the rest of my "Aussie Family" from Kim and Kevin to Leann and Ron and all their clan. A special mention to another lifelong WA resident Glyniss who has never ever missed sending me an annual Christmas card ever since we met in 1982.

Likewise, I can never forget my loving "family" in New Zealand, Alex and Rita Eastwood who have been in my life since 1982. Sadly, the late and great Alex Eastwood my "Kiwi Dad" passed away on the 8th July 2020. He will live on in my heart forever.

Other worldwide family and friends include my close "Brother" Ravi Kukadia in Wasington DC who has been with me on my long postcard journey ever since the early 1980s and has never faltered in his help and support to this day. A very special thank you to my cousin Mahmooda in Melbourne and my ever so missed late lovely cousin Zubaida, once my warm and welcoming shining light in Singapore. I must mention my American "Sister" Shamila from Houston, TX, a lifelong supporter of my works and a truly wonderful host on my many visits to the USA. Her four wonderful sons who have also always looked forward to my latest book, especially since they have visited me in the UK on many occasions with their father Mr T (Tahiree), my close friend since 1982. Continued support from my very nice friends Jujji and Sajji in Dubai and the many friends in Cyprus including Kyriakos Timotheou and family, George and Morrow Harris Bitulas and Americano and wife Marilyn.

I cannot leave these Acknowledgement's without mentioning my very close British Airways friends who ever since my joining the airline in 1978 have been supportive and very proud of me and my postcard collecting. These include Johnny Monaghan, Tony Coombes, (Bambino) Gian Piero Malnatti, John Piggott, Henry Fabrice and Marco, Sij, Tahir, Steve Wyatt, Kate Capel, Paul Neary, Isobel Rodriguez, Antionette Lewis and Thierry Barrass. Finally, a few words to my lovely friend Justine and daughter Alice to say Thank You.

Finally, some valued local friends I cannot forget for their loyal and continued presence in my life. My wonderfully caring, ever so supportive and truly loving friend Sue Martin and husband Ron who are never far away and always ready to help, assist and be on hand whenever I have called upon them. They have never let me down. The real lady that is Coleen Jennings who is a true and sincere friend, one that I am blessed to have in my life. A friend for life and one like no other Alyas Rahim and his charming son Harris are my local bedrock in these surreal times.

My friend Dave Roberts and his son Liam, Durham residents who have been very supportive especially of this book being their home county. Other very close friends such my late friend Raja Asghar and son Adil as well as Paul Evans and son Calvin Rigby, plus Kelly Sanderson, Cori Dales, plus Zoe and Louise from the Dorman Museum are always keen to be the first to see what projects

I am working on and waiting for me to bring them all to a final finished picture postcard book.